A Child's First Library of Learning

Wild Animals

TIME-LIFE BOOKS • ALEXANDRIA, VIRGINIA

Contents

❓ Which Is the Fastest Animal?

ANSWER The cheetah is the fastest land animal. It can reach 70 miles (113 km) per hour over short distances. Next fastest is the pronghorn with a speed of 60 miles (97 km) per hour. The sloth, the slowest, can't stand up so it has to drag itself along.

Sloth: One sixth mile (250 m) per hour

Rhinoceros: 28 miles (45 km) per hour

Bat: 15 miles (24 km) per hour

Cat: 29 miles (47 km) per hour

Child: Seven miles (12 km) per hour

Elephant: 24 miles (39 km) per hour

Wild boar: 29 miles (47 km) per hour

Tortoise: Two miles (3 km) per hour

Sprinter: 25 miles (40 km) per hour

Rat: Six miles (10 km) per hour

Camel: 20 miles (32 km) per hour

Pig: 10 miles (16 km) per hour

Panda: 25 miles (40 km) per hour

Fox: 45 miles (72 km) per hour

Pronghorn: 60 miles (97 km) per hour

Dog: 41 miles (66 km) per hour

Kangaroo: 45 miles (72 km) per hour

Lion: 40 miles (64 km) per hour

Cheetah: 70 miles (113 km) per hour

Wolf: 45 miles (72 km) per hour

Horse: 48 miles (77 km) per hour

Giraffe: 35 miles (56 km) per hour

Hare: 45 miles (72 km) per hour

● **To the Parent**

The cheetah is the fastest land animal. Here its top speed is given as 70 miles (113 km) per hour, but this may vary somewhat according to the method used to measure the speed. Animals do not run at full speed over a fixed distance and the circumstances under which they run vary, so no valid comparison can really be made. Speeds shown here were recorded by various methods and do not constitute an irrefutable comparison.

5

❓ Can All Animals Swim?

ANSWER Most animals are good swimmers. In fact, they can swim from the time they're born. But some animals have to be taught how to swim. This group includes people, gorillas and chimpanzees. Once people learn how to swim, they can swim for long distances if they practice enough.

Rat

Cat

Chimpanzee

Snake

Chimpanzees can't swim.

Me too!

I want to learn how to swim.

Chimpanzee

Gorilla

Sea otter

If people practice they can learn to swim. Starting young is a good idea.

Sloth

Deer

▲ Tigers are good swimmers.

Tiger

Dog

Why Do People Have to Practice Swimming?

Almost all animals can float in the water so that their noses are above the surface. All they have to do is move their legs and they're swimming. But if human beings and chimpanzees let themselves float, their nose stays below the surface and they can't breathe. That's why we have to practice to swim.

● **To the Parent**

Human beings must learn to swim, but most other animals are born with the ability. The bodies of all animals, including humans, are naturally buoyant. With most animals the nose stays above water. This determines whether or not an animal can swim without having to learn how. With their nose above the water, most animals can breathe naturally as they swim. People and apes, however, must learn to swim without taking in water through their nose or mouth.

❓ How Can Cheetahs Run So Fast?

ANSWER Over short distances, the cheetah is the fastest animal on land. The cheetah's speed is due to the special way its body is built. It has a soft backbone that bends easily. That allows this big cat to spring forward in great leaps. The cheetah also has long thin claws on its feet. They work like spikes to grip the ground and help the cheetah run very fast.

◼ How a cheetah runs

The cheetah coils its body like a spring, and its hind legs give a powerful kick.

▼ **Catching a gazelle.** After a top-speed pursuit,

The cheetah's claws stick out from its toes. When it runs they act like spikes on running shoes.

● **To the Parent**

The cheetah, a member of the cat family, pursues its prey with astonishing speed. Every part of the cheetah's body is designed for speed. The supple structure of the bones of its spine, a characteristic of all felines, plays an important part in giving the cheetah its ability to run at great speed. Unlike those of most of the cats, the cheetah's claws cannot be retracted and are always exposed. The cheetah runs in sprints and lacks endurance. For this reason the cheetah pursues its prey for no more than about 600 feet (180 m).

The cheetah stretches out like a spring being released suddenly, and its body leaps forward fully in the air.

A single spring may take it as far as 23 feet (7 m). When its front legs touch the ground it coils its body up again.

the female cheetah overtakes its prey, seizes it by the throat and kills it.

Why Do Tigers Have Stripes?

ANSWER The stripes make the tiger hard to see. Out in the open the tiger's yellow and black stripes are very easy to see. But the tiger becomes harder to see when it's in the bushes or among trees. Deer and other animals can't see colors very well, so that makes it even easier for the tiger to hide.

Is there a tiger in there or not?

▲ The eyes of a deer see only a black-and-white image.

▲ Peering out from a thicket of grass, the tigers blend in with the background.

10

These Markings Are Hard for Other Animals to See

Wildcats and jaguars live in thick brush and grass. This background creates a contrast of light and shadows. Wildcats and jaguars have dark markings on a lighter background which enables them to blend in smoothly with their surroundings, making it difficult for their prey to see them. They can then get close before they're seen.

The Bengal wildcat lives in woods and forests, preying on small animals.

Jaguars live in dense jungle regions, hunting monkeys, peccaries and tapirs.

These markings are hard for enemies to see

Some weak animals that are often targets of attack by enemies have round, white markings. These markings look like the round, white spots made when the sun shines through the trees of the forest. The light and dark patches blend into the background so that the animal can avoid the eyes of its hungry enemies.

When it hides, the fawn's spots help hide it from enemy eyes.

The tapir has a spotted coat when it's young and helpless.

In summer deer have white spots. In winter these spots disappear.

The wild boar has white markings only when it's young.

11

? Did You Know That Male Lions Don't Hunt?

ANSWER Lions live in the wide grasslands of Africa, not in the jungle. Among lions, hunting is left up to the females. The male lions are strong, but they don't help at all with the hunting.

Female lions join together to go hunting. Their light brown fur helps them hide from prey in the dry grass.

Doesn't the Male Lion Need to Eat Anything?

When the female lions bring back something
to eat, the male lion always eats first.

Once the male has finished, the young
lion cubs and the female lions can eat.

When they're young, male lions often
live alone and hunt their own food.

? Why Do Elephants Live in Herds?

ANSWER Elephants form herds or groups made up of only females and their young. The oldest female becomes the leader, and all the others follow her for their protection.

In elephant herds the grandmother is the leader. The father elephant lives alone, apart from the herd.

▲ African elephants.

An elephant herd and the duties of the leader

Even when the weather is dry, the leader knows where to find water and shows the others where to find it.

When an enemy appears, the herd gathers with the young in the center, and the leader comes out to fight.

14

The herd follows the leader, looking for food, water and places to rest. They always follow the same path.

Elephants cooperate for survival. When one of the herd is injured, the others stay close by to give it help.

● **To the Parent**

An elephant herd is composed of females related by blood, plus their young. All the adults are sisters, or mother and daughter. The herd forms extremely close bonds and the members assist one another in many ways. The herd follows a leader, which is the oldest female. She uses her years of experience to assure the safety of the herd as a whole. For example, the leader knows the feeding grounds, watering holes and ways to combat enemies. It is noteworthy that although elephants have a lifespan of about 60 years, such an age is not usual in the wild. Half die by the age of 15, and only about one elephant in five reaches the age of 30. When the young have grown the females remain with the herd, but the males leave to begin an independent life. Only in mating season are the males allowed close to the herd.

? Why Don't Gorillas Hunt Animals?

ANSWER Gorillas are not hunters. They eat only plants. Gorillas are especially fond of fresh grass and tree leaves, but they also like bark and roots. Gorillas travel around in groups called bands, eating only the things they find most delicious. They never attack animals for food.

▲ **Eating leaves.** Since leaves are not very nourishing the gorilla has to eat a lot.

16

How Gorillas Live

Gorillas live in bands that are led by a single male. Because older males have a white back, they are known as silverbacks.

Thump!
Thump!
Thump!
Thump!

When one male meets another male or wants to attract the attention of a female, he may call out and pound his chest.

At night gorillas break off tree branches and cover them with leaves to make nests for sleeping.

Things a gorilla eats

Thistles

Bamboo shoots

Bamboo sprigs

Celery

Raspberries

Catchweed

❓ Did You Know That Pandas Are Very Tiny at Birth?

▲ A mother panda plays with her offspring in a zoo.

ANSWER The baby giant panda is only about as big as a mouse when it's born. It doesn't yet have the black markings adults have, and its eyes aren't yet open, but it can cry in a loud voice.

The newly born panda is covered with soft white fur.

After about three weeks the black markings can be seen.

When four months have gone by it gains in strength and size.

18

Young Pandas Love to Play

Baby pandas like to play ball and to climb trees. They play hard and then take long naps.

▲ Look at me. I can really climb now!

I can chew bamboo leaves ▼ just like Mother. But I'm not old enough to eat really properly just yet.

Look at my ball. It has ▲ the same colors I have.

In the fifth month it can eat soft rice with milk.

After about a year and two months it begins to eat the leaves of the bamboo plant.

Is a Skunk's Terrible Smell Really Strong Enough to Protect It?

ANSWER That awful smell is a very powerful weapon. When another animal attacks it, the skunk sprays its enemy. The smell is so terrible that most other animals are not able to keep on attacking. This is how the small skunk can protect itself from very large enemies.

A spotted skunk stands on its front feet to warn off an enemy.

If the enemy doesn't go away, the skunk sprays it with mist.

The Skunk's Secret

The skunk has glands in its rear end where the foul-smelling liquid is produced. The skunk sprays out a fine mist that smells really bad. It can make the skunk's enemies choke and their eyes tear.

It smells bad, and it makes you cry.

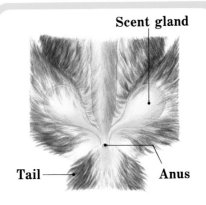

Scent gland

Tail   **Anus**

The scent glands are used to make the liquid that smells so bad.

The eagle owl is the only enemy that will attack a skunk. Even if it's sprayed the owl doesn't seem to mind the smell at all.

Most enemies know how to recognize a skunk and will run away at the sight of one even when they're starving.

These give off an unpleasant smell too

There are also several other creatures that use unpleasant odors to protect themselves from their enemies. Some are large and some are very small.

Ground beetle

Swallowtail caterpillar

Weasel

Stinkbug

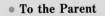

● **To the Parent**

The skunk is a member of the weasel family. It is well known for emitting by far the most offensive odor of all weasels. The source of the smell is a liquid secreted by a pair of glands near the anus. For carnivores with an acute sense of smell, the suffering the odor causes is almost lethal.

How Do Porcupines Protect Themselves?

ANSWER The porcupine's body is covered by long quills that look like needles. These are the porcupine's weapon. The quills are very strong and the tips are extremely sharp. They pierce the skin of any animal unfortunate enough to encounter them.

Most of the time the quills lie flat.

How the porcupine protects itself

When the porcupine first sees an enemy, it makes a rustling sound with its quills to frighten the enemy.

If the enemy doesn't run away, the porcupine backs into it and sticks in the quills. The enemy quickly gives up.

When the quills hit an enemy they easily fall off of the porcupine. But when they stick in the enemy's skin, removing them is difficult. Enemies seldom attack twice.

These have quills too

Spiny anteater   **Hedgehog**

The spiny anteater and hedgehog also have quills, but their quills are somewhat shorter. Unlike the porcupine, these animals do not use their quills to attack enemies. When the spiny anteater and the hedgehog are attacked, they protect themselves by rolling up into small, prickly balls.

● **To the Parent**

About two thirds of the way down its spine, a porcupine has quills from 3 to 15 inches (7.5-40 cm) long, which are the porcupine's fur in different form. They come out when they touch an enemy. The quills have barbs that are very hard to get out when they stick into things. Although the quills are not poisonous, wounds often become infected, causing death to the animal. Recent studies prove that the hedgehog's quills serve not only as a form of defense, but also as a sort of shock absorber to cushion the animal against any injury if it falls out of a tree.

How Does an Eagle Catch Its Food?

ANSWER Eagles have sharp eyes and fly high in the sky looking for prey on the ground below. If an eagle sees the motion of a small bird or animal it dives quickly to try to capture the victim with its sharp claws.

Sharp claws are an eagle's weapons.

The Way an Eagle Hunts And Captures Its Prey

An eagle uses its eyes like binoculars. It can see small things no larger than a speck from far away.

When an eagle spots a rabbit on the ground it dives on the fleeing animal with its sharp claws extended.

When it sees something to eat, it folds its wings back to reduce wind resistance and dives downward.

It grasps the prey using its long, curved claws, and uses its strength to hold it firmly.

❓ Why Does a Leopard Take Its Food up a Tree?

ANSWER Hyenas steal food from other animals but can't climb trees. The leopard takes food up a tree so it can't be stolen by hyenas or other animals. That way a leopard won't be disturbed as it eats.

Spotted hyenas form packs of up to 10 or more animals and try to steal the leopard's food.

The leopard takes its food up onto a tree branch. Hyenas can't climb trees, so the leopard can enjoy a quiet meal.

● To the Parent

The leopard is an expert climber and makes very good use of trees. One use is to hide food in the branches. This is because the leopard must be on constant watch for attacks from packs of hyenas intent on stealing its prey. When the prey is too large to be eaten all at once, the leftovers would likely be found if they were kept at ground level. A tall tree is the natural hiding place. Leopards also sometimes lie in wait in tree branches when they are hunting. They can often be found resting quietly or taking an afternoon nap on a tree branch. Unlike lions, which hunt in groups, the leopard hunts alone, mostly at night, looking for small mammals and birds. It hunts by either lying in wait or creeping up close and springing upon its prey.

A leopard sometimes waits in a tree for prey and springs on its victim from above.

A leopard in a tree with its food ▶

How Does a Bear Catch a Salmon?

ANSWER As salmon swim upriver to lay eggs, bears stand on rocks near the river banks and scoop the fish up with their claws. Bears also wade in the water to catch fish in their mouths.

Bears' claws may be more than 2 inches (5 cm) long.

A bear stands on a rock near a river bank and waits for a salmon to swim close so he can catch it with his claws.

This bear has waded into the river to catch salmon with its sharp canine teeth. Its teeth may be an inch (2.5 cm) or more in length.

● **To the Parent**

The brown bear is one of the larger bears, weighing as much as 1,100 pounds (500 kg). Weights vary depending on where the bear lives. Bears that live where salmon are plentiful grow larger than those living away from rivers. In addition to salmon and trout, brown bears also eat young deer, small mammals, insects, and plant roots or fruit. They may also attack farm animals.

A fresh seafood dinner

Do Killer Whales Really Attack Larger Whales?

ANSWER The killer whale is related to the porpoise as well as to other whales. It eats fish, squid, penguins, seals, sea lions and even porpoises. Most whales travel together in groups called pods. Sometimes a pod of killer whales has been known to attack a much larger whale such as the great blue whale, which is the largest of all mammals.

A pod of killer whales attacking a humpback whale

30

▲ **Male killer whale.** It may be as long as 33 feet (10 m), and its dorsal fin may reach a height of 7 feet (2 m).

● **To the Parent**

Killer whales can be found in oceans all around the globe, but they most frequently live in the middle and higher latitudes. Normally killer whales live in pods ranging in number from four to 40. The members cooperate in hunting, driving schools of salmon or trout into shallow waters. The advantage of moving in pods is obvious when killer whales try to attack larger whales.

How Can Owls Catch Animals in the Dark?

ANSWER Owls have very good eyes and ears. That's why they're able to catch animals at night. Owls can see even when there's only very little light. Their hearing is so sharp that just by listening they can tell where their prey is and which way it's running. Even on the darkest nights with no light at all, owls can catch their prey simply by listening.

● **To the Parent**

The success of owls in hunting at night is due to their exceptionally keen senses of sight and hearing. Some species that hunt late at night can tell the position of their prey with great accuracy by sound alone. These species have feathers on their faces that act as sound collectors to amplify even the faintest noises. The owl's ears are positioned asymmetrically to help it pinpoint the exact position and direction of its prey.

The masked owl is alert during the night. Even in pitch dark it can tell just from the sound in which direction its prey is running. If the prey tries to escape by changing direction, the owl can still follow and then swoop down and capture it.

How Can Bats Catch Insects Even on the Darkest Night?

ANSWER Bats make sounds that are much too high for us to hear. The sounds travel in invisible waves through the night sky. When the waves strike a flying insect, the sound bounces back, or echoes. The bat hears this with its huge ears. It's like radar.

■ **Bats make high-pitched sounds that travel in ultrasonic waves**

Ultrasonic waves from the nose

Bats that send out ultrasonic waves from their nose use a narrow beam that sweeps back and forth like a searchlight.

Ultrasonic waves from the mouth

Bats that send ultrasonic waves from their mouth give off pulses that spread out over a wide area in front of them.

● **To the Parent**

The method that bats use to pinpoint the position of prey using ultrasonic echoes is called echo location. Because of their high frequency, ultrasonic waves are reflected even from objects as small as an insect. Sound that is audible to humans has long wavelengths that do not bounce back very well from small objects. Bats rely on the reflected ultrasonic waves to navigate and to determine the size, direction, speed and position of their prey.

A bat catching moths ▶

This kind of bat sends out ultrasonic waves from its nose to find moths in the dark. Notice the peculiar shape of the bat's nose.

How Does a Kingfisher Catch Its Food?

ANSWER The kingfisher is a bird that catches fish for food. Hovering above water, it looks for small fish. When it sees something it likes it folds its wings back and dives into the water. Under the water it quickly uses its beak to catch the fish.

From above ▶ it watches for a fish to catch.

▲ It dives headfirst into the water.

▲ With its beak it makes the catch.

Membranes protect its eyes under the water.

▲ With the fish in its mouth the kingfisher comes out of the water.

■ When the kingfisher swallows a fish

The kingfisher turns the fish around so that it will go down headfirst.

Tailfirst, it would get caught.

If the fish went in tailfirst, it would catch in the throat.

● **To the Parent**

The kingfisher can hover in midair. When it spots a fish it wants it dives into the water. When it hits the water the two wings are folded back into a wedge. This shape minimizes water resistance so the force of the dive is not dissipated. The moment it grabs the fish in its beak it spreads its wings which act as a brake to stop the dive. While the bird is under the water its eyes are covered by protective membranes.

How Do Polar Bears Live In a Land of Ice and Snow?

ANSWER Most polar bears live alone and wander over floating sheets of ice in search of their prey. Their main source of food is seals.

The seal has made a hole in the ice so it can breathe. The polar bear waits beside the hole and catches the seal when it comes up for fresh air.

Polar bears live in the far north on the islands and along the cold seacoast of the Arctic Ocean.

38

The Polar Bear's Special Fur

Polar bears are completely covered with a coat of white fur which blends in well with the white of the ice and snow so prey can't easily see them.

Polar bears have fur growing on their paws. This makes it easy for them to walk or run across fields of ice and snow without the danger of slipping.

Their white coat keeps the heat from escaping. They also have a thick undercoat of fur so they stay warm and comfortable in the worst cold.

In November or December a mother polar bear digs a deep hole in a snowdrift for her den. A month or two later she gives birth to two or three cubs, and they sleep snugly in the den with her until spring comes. The bear cubs stay with their mother for about two years after they're born so that she can feed and care for them.

Polar bears are very good swimmers and can stay in the water for hours. Water doesn't soak through their fur, so they don't get wet to the skin or lose body heat even when it's freezing cold.

● To the Parent

The second largest land carnivore, a polar bear may weigh 1,600 pounds (725 kg). The white coat provides camouflage and protection from the cold. The white hairs are hollow and give the bear protection by retaining almost all of its body heat. Beneath these hairs the animal has a plush undercoat of fur to keep it warm. The polar bear's principal source of food is the seals it attacks in their breathing holes or out on the ice pack.

? Why Do Rhinoceroses Have Horns?

ANSWER They use their horns for protection. Rhinoceroses are known to be very strong and are not often attacked by their enemies. When something threatens a young rhinoceros, which is still very weak, the mother fights for it.

The Rhinoceros's Secret

Rhinoceroses don't have sharp eyes. They're nearsighted, which means they can't see far.

They have sensitive ears and a keen sense of smell. With them they watch out for enemies.

Adult rhinoceroses are very strong. Not even a lion would dare to attack these powerful animals.

She tosses the enemy on her horn.

● **To the Parent**

There are five species of rhinoceroses in the world. The Indian rhinoceros and the Java rhinoceros have only one horn. All the other species have two. The species most commonly displayed in zoos is the black rhinoceros from Africa. In spite of their strength rhinoceroses are in danger of extinction. Although hunting them is against the law, poachers kill them for their horns, which are still used in parts of Asia to prepare certain potions.

❓ Why Do Rattlesnakes Make a Rattling Sound?

ANSWER Rattlesnakes use their rattles to scare their enemies. The snakes have a poisonous bite. They can use their poison to kill small animals to eat. But they make a rattling sound to scare away humans and other large animals. The snakes are afraid they might be hurt or killed themselves.

How they make their tails rattle

The rattle on the end of a rattlesnake's tail is made of skin. Like all snakes, rattlesnakes shed their skin as they grow. This is called molting. When the rattlesnake molts, the old skin that remains becomes a rattle. When the snake shakes its tail, the dry skin makes a sound very much like a baby rattle. When a rattlesnake is hatched it hasn't molted so it has no rattles at all. You can tell the age of a rattlesnake by the number of rattles, one for each time it has molted.

Skin remaining after molting

Skin from the second molting

Tip of the tail

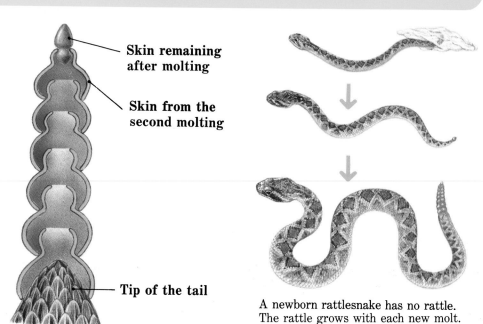

A newborn rattlesnake has no rattle. The rattle grows with each new molt.

▲ **A rattlesnake.** It raises its tail and shakes its rattle made of folds of molted skin.

 ## Doesn't the Sound of the Rattle Warn the Rattlesnake's Prey?

When rattlesnakes hunt, they don't make any noise. They approach their prey very quietly. To do this they keep their tails lifted up and off the ground to make sure they don't make any noise with their rattles.

● **To the Parent**

When any large creature approaches, a rattlesnake will make a noise with the rattle on the tip of its tail. Most animals, including humans, stay clear because they know what makes the noise. The rattlesnake is highly poisonous, but it can be killed easily if it is bitten by a coyote or trampled by a large animal. The snake sounds its distinctive warning to avoid such dangers.

How Does a Scorpion Sting?

ANSWER A scorpion's stinger has poison in it. To kill its prey the scorpion uses the stinger to shoot poison into the animal. There are more than 600 kinds of scorpions in the world. Only a few of them can harm a person. A scorpion that lives in Africa's Sahara is one of the most poisonous. Another dangerous scorpion lives in the southwestern United States.

There is a poison sac inside the tail. The poison flows out of the tail through the sharply pointed tip.

Wow! That thing looks dangerous!

Only a few scorpions can hurt you. But just to be safe, you shouldn't try to pick one up.

When a scorpion is ready to sting its prey it brings the tail up over its back and extends the sting from the tip.

● **To the Parent**

The scorpion normally inhabits tropical and subtropical regions where it is warm all year round. The scorpion's two large claws are used for holding prey, but its poisonous sting is an even more formidable weapon. The scorpion uses its sting on spiders, grasshoppers and similar insects. More than 600 scorpion species exist worldwide, but only a few are able to kill a human being.

Why Do Hippopotamuses Always Stay in the Water?

ANSWER The hippopotamus has skin that's thinner than other animals' skin. This means moisture is lost very easily. If a hippopotamus didn't keep itself wet, its body would dry out, and then it would die. The hippopotamus stays under the water's surface all day to stay wet. Its eyes, nose and ears are near the top of its head so it can stay almost completely underwater.

▲ **A hippopotamus herd.** In the daytime hippopotamuses stay in the water and take things very easy.

A Day in the Life of a Hippopotamus

It stays cool and wet in the water all day.

In the evening it comes up onto the land.

Daytime	Evening
Morning	Night

In the morning it goes back into the water.

During the night it feeds on grass and other plants.

Hippopotamuses like to eat grass on land. They always take the same path to their feeding grounds.

● **To the Parent**

Since the skin of the hippopotamus is extremely thin, moisture is easily lost, so it stays under water all day. Otherwise it would suffer from dehydration. The nostrils and ears of the hippopotamus can be closed so that water does not enter when the animal submerges. The hippopotamus moves with great agility in the water and can submerge to depths of more than 35 feet (11 m). It can stay down for periods of five minutes or more.

Why Do Wolves Howl?

ANSWER   Wolves live in groups called packs.
Each pack has its own territory where
it hunts for food and raises its young.
Wolves howl to tell other wolf packs
where their territory is. When wolves
hear this howling, they usually don't
enter the other wolf pack's territory.
If they do enter, there's a fight.

How Wolves Live

Each wolf pack has a leader. All the wolves in the pack know which wolf is the leader that they must follow.

Wolves hunt in packs. They're able to catch prey because all of the members of the pack cooperate in the hunt.

In spring the wolf cubs are born. They're raised not only by their own mother but by all the wolves in the pack.

● **To the Parent**

Normally wolves form packs of about 15 animals. A pack may have territory measuring 6 to 12 miles (10 to 20 km) in diameter. Wolves howl to protect that territory. All members of the pack howl together and the sound carries as far as six miles (10 km). Sometimes one pack may howl in response to the howling of another. If their response is weak, they run the risk of being attacked. Wolves howl more in the winter when the mating season begins, but lone wolves do not respond to the howling.

49

Why Do Hyenas Eat Other Animals' Food?

ANSWER Hyenas eat leftovers from animals that lions have killed, and they eat other dead animals too. That kind of meat is called carrion. It's not always rotten. But even if it is, hyenas can eat it. They don't get sick because their bodies are not harmed by germs in rotting food.

Are Leftovers the Only Things Hyenas Eat?

▲ **On the attack.** Spotted hyenas normally hunt at night, but this photograph shows a rare daylight hunt.

The striped hyena and the brown hyena actually live on nothing but dead meat left by other animals. But the spotted hyena not only eats carrion; it hunts for itself. It may even attack a pride of lions and try to steal their food.

▲ **Striped hyena.** It roams far in search of food.

Spotted hyenas will steal food from a leopard or a cheetah.

51

? What Do Rabbits Eat During the Winter?

ANSWER From spring through autumn rabbits eat different kinds of grasses. When winter comes and the fields and mountains are covered with snow they eat dry grass, dry leaves, the buds on trees, bark, roots and twigs.

▲ **Rabbit chewing a twig**

I wish this tasted better!

Leaf buds

Leaves

Bark

■ Feet for walking on snow

Strange!

Rabbits have hair on their paws so that they can walk on deep snow without sinking into it.

■ Sleeping on top of the snow

Rabbits often sleep in hollows in the snow on the sunny southern slope of a hill.

What Do the Other Animals Do in Winter?

Some animals hibernate during the winter while others continue to move about.

Dormouse
It hibernates.

Monkey

Fox

Field mouse

Rabbit

Raccoon. It sometimes hibernates if it lives in a place where the winters are very severe.

Monkeys, foxes and field mice stay active in the winter.

Snakes and lizards
They like to sleep in holes.

I nap too.

● **To the Parent**

Rabbits normally eat the leaves of evergreens and other tender plants like chickweed or dandelion. But in the winter many plants die out or are covered with snow. Rabbits must then eat anything they can find, like the bark of trees. They can survive the winter eating nothing but bark or dead leaves.

53

❓ What Do Boars Use Their Noses For?

ANSWER These relatives of common pigs and hogs can't see things very well. Instead they have a very good sense of smell. They can detect things from distances of up to 1,600 feet (500 m). Wild boars may also use their sensitive nose to look for food under the ground. When a wild boar finds something good to eat, such as a tender young root, it can dig it out with its sharply pointed tusks and tough snout.

Wild boars can sniff out food that's under the ground.

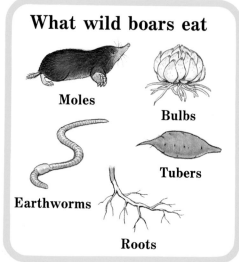

What wild boars eat

Moles

Bulbs

Earthworms

Tubers

Roots

The boar's long snout is very useful when it wants to dig up food from under the ground. Its snout is extremely tough and strong so the boar can dig very fast.

54

How a Wild Boar Lives

In spring the female wild boar normally has four to six babies. They stay with their mother from spring right through to winter, but about the end of winter they go off alone. Wild boars will eat anything. We call such animals omnivores. Wild boars look for food in the forest and sometimes in farmers' fields.

▲ **Eating grass.** It will eat just a little because this is not really a favorite.

▲ Boars have white markings until they're about six months old.

▲ Wild boars are very good swimmers.

▲ Wild boars like being in the water very much.

Why Are There No Feathers On a Vulture's Head?

ANSWER Vultures feed on the flesh of dead animals, called carrion. This meat often rots and has germs. If the vulture's head had feathers they would get covered with germs when it ate. Since it is bald the head stays clean.

If a vulture's head got dirty, germs would grow.

The rays of the sun dry the head and the germs soon die.

▲ **Pecking at carrion.** Vultures eat dead animals and prey killed by lions.

A vulture looks for a dead animal, ▼ which it will swoop down to eat.

▲ Some vultures have fuzzy heads.

● **To the Parent**

The lack of feathers on the vulture's head is also an adaptation found on other carrion birds such as the condor and the adjutant stork. If there were feathers on these birds' heads they would have trouble keeping them clean. The vulture's diet may include garbage and rotten meat. Its preference, however, is for animals that have just died, often the prey of lions.

? How Does a Flying Squirrel Fly?

ANSWER The flying squirrel doesn't really fly. It spreads out a flap of skin, or membrane, that stretches from its front legs to its back legs. This lets it glide on air currents. That's also how hang gliders work.

Let's race!

▼ A giant flying squirrel glides through the air at night.

Gliding From Tree to Tree

The giant flying squirrel glides from high in one tree to low in another.

Once it finds a place it would like to land it jumps into the air.

It glides on its membrane.

It climbs a tree.

It grabs the branch with its claws when it lands.

Then it climbs higher in the tree and looks around for the next landing.

Other animals that glide using membranes

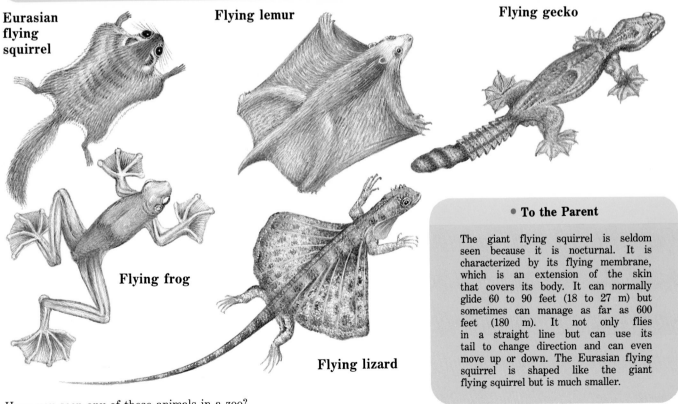

Eurasian flying squirrel

Flying lemur

Flying gecko

Flying frog

Flying lizard

Have you seen any of these animals in a zoo?

❓ Is It True That Moles Will Die If They See the Sun?

ANSWER Moles live in holes that they dig under the ground. They very seldom appear on the surface. Even if they do come out and see the sun they won't die. Moles have such poor eyesight that they can barely detect light.

Moles can really tell only whether it's light or dark. They can't see much else.

■ The mole's body

The front legs are like shovels so the mole can dig in the earth.

❓ Why Do People Say a Mole Will Die in Sunlight?

No one knows how people got the idea that a mole will die if it gets into the sunlight. People have many wrong ideas about animals. The truth is that moles must eat constantly. They can die if they go without food for as few as three hours. It could be that someone who had caught a mole forgot to feed it and the mole died. It would be easy to guess that being in the sun was the reason that the mole had died. Or maybe people got the idea from seeing moles that had come up above ground and had died.

Moles like eating earthworms.

What would happen if a mole was caught by someone who then forgot to feed it?

Moles can hear, but you can't tell that they have earholes.

Their fur is very soft like velvet.

The tail is very small.

■ The mole's secrets

Moles have very flexible bodies. A mole can turn around when it wants to, even in a narrow tunnel.

Moles have very sharp noses and are good at sniffing out earthworms in the ground.

Before a mole eats an earthworm it squeezes the dirt in the body of the earthworm down toward the tail. Next it starts eating at the head. When it's half finished it starts again at the tail. That way all the dirt in the worm can be squeezed out.

If the mole wasn't given any food to eat for three hours or more it would starve to death.

● **To the Parent**

The body of the mole is adapted to life underground. The forelegs, which are used for digging, are shaped like shovels. The ears, which could get in the way, are atrophied. Since it lives in a world of darkness the eyes are also atrophied and hidden under membranes. Thus if a mole were to see the sun it would be able to tell only that it was bright. Sunlight would not kill the mole. But because it must eat constantly it could easily starve to death if it were put in a cage.

61

❓Do Giraffes Make Sounds?

ANSWER Have you ever heard a giraffe in the zoo making a noise? Probably not. The giraffe is an animal that almost never calls out. But sometimes the call of a giraffe may be heard.

Vocal cords

The throat has the vocal cords needed to make a sound.

The giraffe doesn't say very much, does it?

To the stomach

To the lungs

Vocal cords

Animals can make noises because they have vocal cords. People can talk because they have them.

When Do Giraffes Cry Out?

Giraffes seldom call out although they can make several different noises. They can make a kind of growling sound. They also make a funny noise with their noses. They make these noises when they feel hungry, when the mother and father call to each other or when they see an enemy. Baby giraffes make a kind of squeaking sound.

▲ **Male and female giraffes in the wild**

They call when they feel hungry.

● **To the Parent**

For a long time people thought that the giraffe was voiceless, but in recent years observers have recorded a variety of cries and calls. These cries seem to be of two types. One is an emotional cry and may indicate for instance that the animal is unhappy, surprised or lonely. The other type of cry is for communication, to warn other giraffes of the presence of an enemy, for example. Giraffes' cries are mostly of the emotional type. They seldom cry out to communicate with the herd.

They also call if they see an enemy.

❓ Do Snakes Have Ears?

ANSWER Snakes don't have ears that you can see. They don't have earholes either. So you'd never know from looking at a snake that it has ears. But snakes do have a kind of ear that's inside their head. It's located near the lower jaw.

How do you keep your glasses on?

▲ **Snake's head.** You can see the eyes, the nose and the mouth, but can you see any ears?

Does That Mean They Can't Hear Anything?

A snake can hear noises but not very well. It doesn't hear noises coming through the air as humans do. What a snake can hear is vibrations that come through the ground. These sound waves pass from the ground to the bones of the jaw and then to the bones of the ear. That's the way the snake picks up sounds.

Animals that seem to have no ears

There are many animals that don't appear to have ears but that really do have them.

Mole. It doesn't have outside ears.

Lizard. There are small earholes just behind the lizard's eyes.

Porpoise. It hears sounds through its lower jaw.

Bird. It has ears hidden below the cheek feathers.

Frog. The ears of a frog are below and to the side of the eyes. You can even see the frog's eardrums.

● **To the Parent**

Snakes do not appear to have ears. Their external ear structures and the earholes have entirely disappeared. Because the inner ear still exists they are able to hear noises, however imperfectly. Snakes can hear only low vibrations because only a single bone is connected to the jawbone to transmit sounds to the inner ear.

What's the Largest Poisonous Snake?

ANSWER The largest poisonous snake in the world is the king cobra, which lives in India and Southeast Asia. Because it's so big it has a lot of poison. The poison is strong, and the king cobra's bite can kill an elephant.

An elephant can die if it is bitten by a king cobra.

◀ **King cobra.** It lives in India and Southeast Asia. Sometimes it is as long as 18 feet (5.5 m). An angry king cobra swells up its throat, forming a hood. This snake is dangerous if it's angry or hungry.

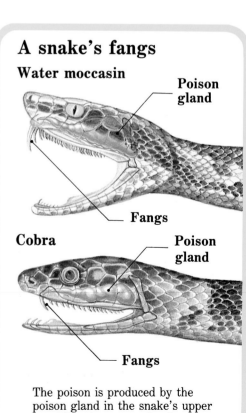

A snake's fangs

Water moccasin

Poison gland

Fangs

Cobra

Poison gland

Fangs

The poison is produced by the poison gland in the snake's upper jaw. Then it goes to the fangs.

What Happens When a Poisonous Snake Bites?

Snakes use two kinds of poison. One kind attacks the nervous system. The other causes pain and swelling.

> If you're bitten by a snake it doesn't mean you'll die, but you should go to a hospital right away. They have medicine for snakebites.

■ How do people recognize a nerve-poison snakebite?

The coral snake, cobra and some other snakes use nerve poison. Their bite isn't especially painful, but after a while the victim is unable to move. Then the victim can't breathe. That's because the poison goes to the nerves and the brain.

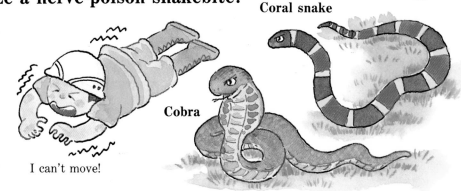

Coral snake

Cobra

I can't move!

■ How do people recognize a blood-poison snakebite?

The pit viper and other vipers use a blood poison. Their bites are very painful and quickly cause swelling. When the poison moves through the body the muscles and organs are poisoned.

The bite hurts a lot and it swells.

Water moccasin

Okinawa viper

Unusual poisonous snakes

An African spitting cobra can spit poison into the eye of its enemy.

Spitting cobra

Rattlesnake

The rattlesnake, which lives in North America, makes noise with a rattle on its tail to scare its enemies.

● **To the Parent**

King cobras are the largest poisonous snakes in the world. They can reach 18 feet (5.5 m) in length. They are usually placid and do not attack unless cornered. A snakebite does not mean that death is inevitable. The victim can often be saved if the appropriate antivenin is injected in time. Be sure to remind your child that most of the snakes in the world are quite harmless.

How Can a Mongoose Defeat a Cobra?

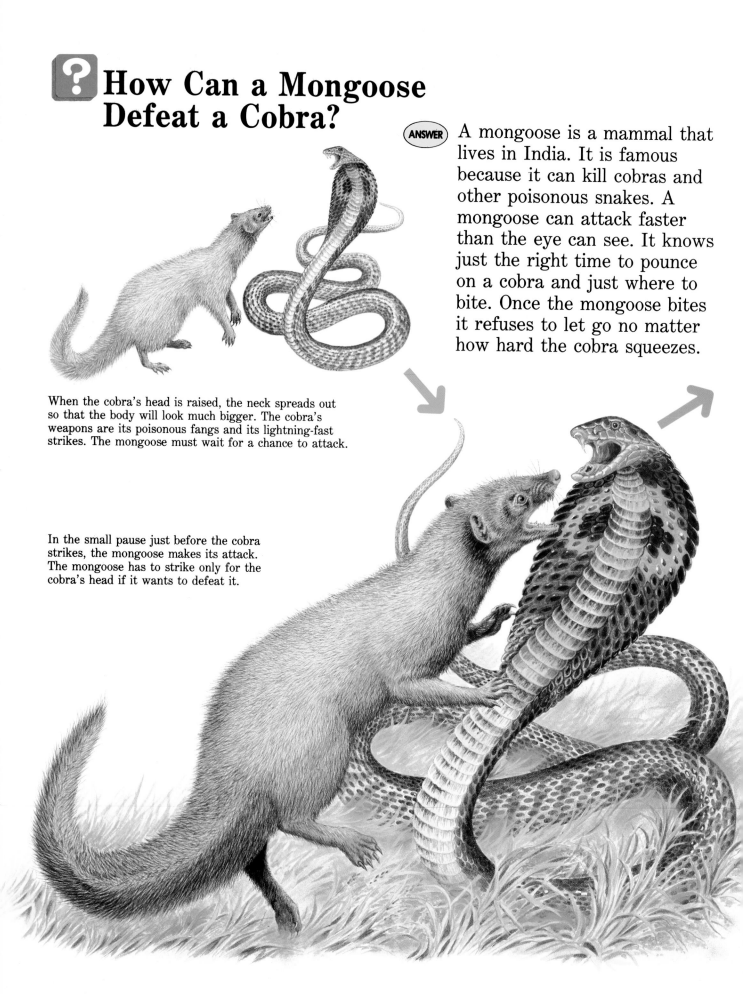

ANSWER A mongoose is a mammal that lives in India. It is famous because it can kill cobras and other poisonous snakes. A mongoose can attack faster than the eye can see. It knows just the right time to pounce on a cobra and just where to bite. Once the mongoose bites it refuses to let go no matter how hard the cobra squeezes.

When the cobra's head is raised, the neck spreads out so that the body will look much bigger. The cobra's weapons are its poisonous fangs and its lightning-fast strikes. The mongoose must wait for a chance to attack.

In the small pause just before the cobra strikes, the mongoose makes its attack. The mongoose has to strike only for the cobra's head if it wants to defeat it.

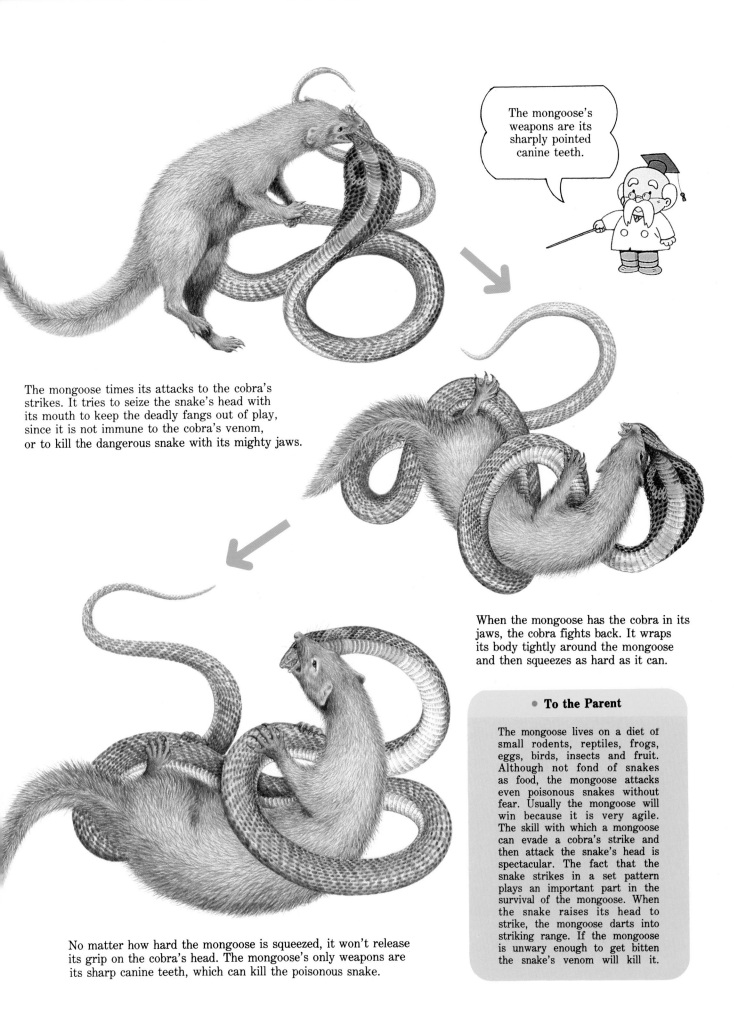

The mongoose's weapons are its sharply pointed canine teeth.

The mongoose times its attacks to the cobra's strikes. It tries to seize the snake's head with its mouth to keep the deadly fangs out of play, since it is not immune to the cobra's venom, or to kill the dangerous snake with its mighty jaws.

When the mongoose has the cobra in its jaws, the cobra fights back. It wraps its body tightly around the mongoose and then squeezes as hard as it can.

No matter how hard the mongoose is squeezed, it won't release its grip on the cobra's head. The mongoose's only weapons are its sharp canine teeth, which can kill the poisonous snake.

● **To the Parent**

The mongoose lives on a diet of small rodents, reptiles, frogs, eggs, birds, insects and fruit. Although not fond of snakes as food, the mongoose attacks even poisonous snakes without fear. Usually the mongoose will win because it is very agile. The skill with which a mongoose can evade a cobra's strike and then attack the snake's head is spectacular. The fact that the snake strikes in a set pattern plays an important part in the survival of the mongoose. When the snake raises its head to strike, the mongoose darts into striking range. If the mongoose is unwary enough to get bitten the snake's venom will kill it.

Do Piranhas Attack People?

ANSWER The piranha is known for its very sharp teeth. Stories are told of people who go into a river full of piranhas and are attacked by these meat-eaters. In fact piranhas do not normally attack people. They prefer small fish or animals that are injured or weakened. Usually when a person is in water near a piranha the fish will swim away and hide.

Normally piranhas won't attack people.

▲ **The dusky piranha.** Its razor-sharp teeth and powerful jaws are the piranha's fearsome weapons.

How Piranhas Live

Piranhas eat meat. If they see a fish that's weak they will attack even if it's another piranha.

▲ When the red-bellied piranha is young it has a distinctive red marking like blood on its belly.

If a weak or injured animal falls into a river or moves in a strange way piranhas attack right away.

Most fish just lay eggs and leave them alone, but the male piranha stays nearby to guard them.

■ Some types of piranhas don't eat meat

The wimpled piranha brushes against other fish and eats their scales.

Some piranhas live mainly on water plants, not on meat.

● **To the Parent**

The piranha is actually a rather timid creature. If a person goes into a river that is inhabited by piranhas the fish generally hide among the water plants. Sometimes a curious piranha may nudge the person but normally piranhas do not attack. Their teeth, however, are extremely sharp, and a large animal can be quickly reduced to a skeleton. Some people like to keep piranhas as decorative fish, but one should never put a hand or finger into an aquarium with piranhas. The result could be a severe injury or loss of a finger.

71

How Do Koalas Look After Their Young?

ANSWER When a koala is born it crawls into its mother's pouch right away. It stays there as it grows and gets its mother's milk right inside the pouch. When the baby is big enough to come out the mother carries it on her back.

As soon as it's born the baby crawls into a pouch on the mother's stomach.

Baby koalas are always carried around by their mothers.

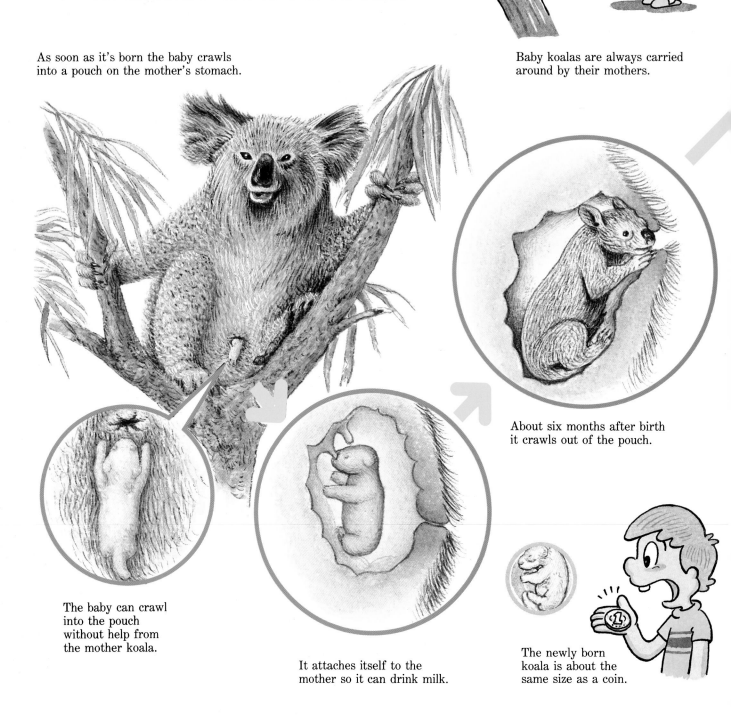

The baby can crawl into the pouch without help from the mother koala.

It attaches itself to the mother so it can drink milk.

About six months after birth it crawls out of the pouch.

The newly born koala is about the same size as a coin.

The Koala's Secret

About the time this little Australian marsupial stops drinking milk, its mother begins to feed it on a diet of eucalyptus leaves she has half eaten.

When the mother koala jumps from one tree to another her baby holds onto her fur tightly.

When it can first leave the pouch it crawls in and out for about two months.

Don't you feel cold?

When it rains the mother koala wraps herself around the baby so that it doesn't get wet and catch cold.

The mother carries the baby around on her back once it's too big to get into the pouch.

73

Why Do Alligators Bury Their Eggs?

(ANSWER) That's how they get them to hatch. Saltwater crocodiles and the American alligator build nests near the water and lay eggs in them. Then the mother covers them with a big mound of vegetation 8 to 10 feet (2½ to 3 m) wide and 40 inches (1 m) high. Heat produced by the decaying vegetation makes the eggs hatch. The mother will guard the eggs for the three months it takes them to hatch.

▲ **American alligator.** It lives in the swamps, ponds and rivers of the southeastern United States.

The temperature inside is about 85° F. (30° C.).

A female guarding her nest of eggs

And Then What Happens When the Eggs Hatch?

The mother alligator hears the babies crying after they hatch, and she breaks open the nest so they can get out.

The mother alligator picks up the babies as they come out of the nest and carries them to the water.

The temperature makes the babies male or female

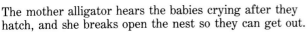

The sex of ordinary alligators is determined by the temperature of the eggs in the nest seven to 21 days after they're laid. All the babies will be females if it's 85° F. (30° C.) or below. If it's 93° F. (34° C.) or more, the babies will be males.

Nests that are farther away from the water are warmer, so all the babies are male.

Nests that are near water are cooler.
In this case, all the babies are female.

• To the Parent

Most species of alligator guard and protect their eggs. Both the saltwater crocodile and the American alligator do this by building large nests in the form of a tall mound of vegetation. These nests not only protect the eggs but warm them with the heat generated by decomposition and solar energy.

? What Is a Gavial?

A short, broad alligator snout

ANSWER A gavial is a relative of the alligator and the crocodile. This reptile lives in India. It looks different from an alligator because it feeds on different animals. An alligator catches water birds and slower-moving animals in its strong jaws. A gavial catches small, fast-moving fish. Its narrow snout helps it move quickly through the water.

A long, thin gavial snout

▲ **Swallowing a fish.** The gavial must hold the fish in its snout so that the fish goes down headfirst.

How a Gavial Catches a Fish

When a fish comes close the gavial swings its thin snout sideways to catch it. The gavial always swallows the fish headfirst so the fins will not catch in its throat.

The gavial's snout is similar to tweezers.

How gavials are born

The mother gavial digs a hole in the sand of a river bank as a nest and lays about 50 eggs. She doesn't always stay where she laid the eggs but visits sometimes to see how things are going. Finally the young hatch and burrow out through the sand. The babies look like adults except that they are only about 12 inches (30 cm) long.

▲ **A gavial hatching.** It breaks the shell of its egg to get out.

This is how a baby gavial breaks out of its shell, but it does it under the sand.

● **To the Parent**

The long, thin snout of the Indian gavial is adapted to a diet of fish. In addition to Indian gavials there are other fish-eating relatives of the crocodile such as the African long-nosed crocodile and the Malayan gavial. All have long, thin snouts which provide less resistance to water and can be moved about quickly.

❓ What Are They Doing?

◀ Two male kangaroos are fighting. Kangaroos support themselves on their tails and kick at their opponent with their legs. Some people think this looks like boxing.

▲ **Indian rhinoceros**

◀ This Indian rhinoceros is taking a bath. These animals love the water and will wallow in a swamp for hours with only the horn and ears showing above the surface.

◀ A spiny anteater has rolled up into a ball. The spiny anteater has hundreds of quills on its back that are like very sharp needles. When it's rolled into a ball like this, it's very hard for an enemy to try to attack.

▲ These wild boars seem to be playing in the mud. But actually the boars are wallowing there to get rid of the insects living on their hair and skin.

▲ A wart hog with an itchy rear end is scratching itself on a rock. If its back itches the wart hog will roll over and scratch itself against the rock.

I just can't reach it.

● To the Parent

The spiny anteater is an extremely primitive mammal that lives in Australia. It is very unusual because it lays eggs, and when they hatch it feeds the young on milk. Although it is only a distant relative, the hedgehog looks similar and also has quills for fur. The places where boars bathe in the mud are called wallows.

? Whose Tail Is This?

■ A cheetah's

The tip of a cheetah's tail is white. Because it's easy to see, the mother uses it to signal her young so they won't stray.

■ A lion's

The lion's tail has a tuft of hair on the tip. The lion uses it to brush away horseflies and other bothersome insects.

■ A tiger's

The tiger's tail has stripes like those on its body. The tail helps the tiger keep its balance when it runs after prey and makes quick turns.

80

Growing-Up Album

Which Top Goes Where?

Here we see some children wearing the bottom half of animal suits. Which top part should each of them put on? Try helping the children find the right top so they can play animals.

Panda

Rabbit

Kangaroo

Panda (3rd child from the right). Rabbit (2nd child from the right). Kangaroo (2nd child from the left).

Lion

Elephant

Giraffe

Lion (child on the left).

Elephant (child on the right).

Giraffe (3rd child from the left).

Which Markings Are Which?

The coat markings numbered from 1 to 6 are all taken from the six animals shown below. They may seem to match, but if you look closely you will see that something is different. See how long it will take you to find out which coat goes with which animal.

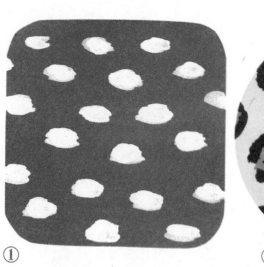

①

②

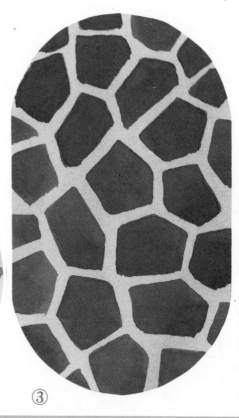

③

Leopard

Deer

Tiger

④

⑤

⑥

Cheetah

Giraffe

Jaguar

1. Deer 2. Jaguar 3. Giraffe 4. Tiger 5. Cheetah 6. Leopard

What's Wrong Here?

Here we see pictures of several animals. If you look closely you'll see that there's something wrong with all of them. Can you see what's funny about each one?

Elephant

Kangaroo

Panda

Giraffe

Tiger

Penguin

Lion

Gorilla

Rhinoceros

The elephant's trunk should be much longer. The kangaroo's tail should curl only slightly and be much longer. The panda's black and white markings are reversed. The giraffe's neck is too short. The tiger's stripes should be up and down. The penguin's beak is too big and too long. The lion should not have horns. The gorilla shouldn't have a tail. The rhinoceros shouldn't have a horn between its ears.

A Child's First Library of Learning

Wild Animals

Time-Life Books Inc. is a wholly owned subsidiary of
Time Incorporated.
Time-Life Books, Alexandria, Virginia
Children's Publishing

Director: Robert H. Smith
Associate Director: R. S. Wotkyns III
Editorial Director: Neil Kagan
Promotion Director: Kathleen Tresnak
Editorial Consultants: Jacqueline A. Ball
                         Andrew Gutelle

Editorial Supervision by:
International Editorial Services Inc.
Tokyo, Japan

Editor: C. E. Berry
Associate Editor: Winston S. Priest
Writer: Edwin Causa
Editorial Assistants: Nobuko Abe
                         Christine Alaimo
                         Dori Ahana

**TIME
LIFE** ®

Library of Congress Cataloging in Publication Data
Wild animals.
    p.   cm. — (A Child's first library of learning)
    Summary: Questions and answers provide information
on the behavior and life cycles of such animals as giraffes,
leopards, skunks, elephants, and alligators. Includes charts,
diagrams, and an activities section.
    ISBN 0-8094-4877-7.   ISBN 0-8094-4878-5 (lib. bdg.)
    1. Animals—Miscellanea—Juvenile literature.   [1. Animals—
Miscellanea.   2. Questions and answers.]   I. Time-Life Books.
II. Series.
QL49.W538 1989   591—dc20   89-4541
©1989 Time-Life Books Inc.
©1983 Gakken Co. Ltd.

Third printing 1992. Printed in U.S.A.
Published simultaneously in Canada.

TIME-LIFE is a trademark of Time Warner Inc. U.S.A.